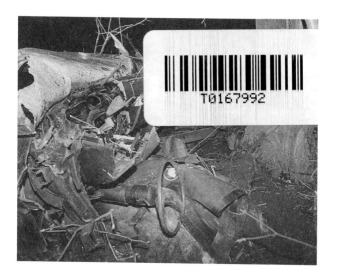

DON'T BE STUPID

Alcohol is a dangerous drug. And, like it or not, it's an illegal drug in America if you're under 21.

Alcohol will severely impair your reflexes, and if you try to drive when you're drunk, you stand a good chance of killing yourself or murdering someone else. Here's a sickening statistic: Among people age 16-24, alcohol-related car wrecks are the **leading cause of death**.

Don't be stupid. Don't abuse alcohol. Don't drink and drive, and don't let your friends drink and drive, either. Use the designated driver system, or call a cab, or something.

Look, if you want to kill yourself, do everyone a favor and play with a toaster in the bathtub. Just don't drive drunk.

The
HANGOVER HANDBOOK

*101 Cures for Humanity's
Oldest Malady*

NIC VAN OUDTSHOORN

Mustang Publishing Co.
Memphis, TN

Published in the USA by arrangement with Beercan
Books, an imprint of Maximedia Pty. of Australia.

Distributed to bookstores by National Book Network.

Cartoons by Shane Summerton.

Library of Congress CIP Data

Van Oudtshoorn, Nic.
    The hangover handbook : 101 cures for
humanity's oldest malady / Nic Van Oudtshoorn. --
Rev. ed.
        p.   cm.
    ISBN 0-914457-90-X (alk. paper)
    1. Hangover cures. 2. Hangover cures--Humor.
    I. Title.
TX951.V364   1997
641.8'74--dc21   97-27788
                                      CIP

Printed in Singapore.
10 9 8 7 6 5 4 3 2 1

Contents

What is a hangover?

 The dictionary defines a hangover as "the after-effects of excessive indulgence in alcoholic drink". But that, as any sufferer will testify, is most inadequate to describe the agonies you suffer after the joys of the night before: Vesuvius erupting in your stomach, a bass drummer thumping on your brain, and a canary fouling its nest in your throat.

Here's a much better definition, supplied by a seasoned sufferer: *You've got a hangover if, after a heavy night on the tiles, you hear the cat walking across the carpet, forcing you to yell out: "Do you have to wake me by stamping your feet?"*

Is a hangover physical or mental? A University of Oklahoma professor, Dr Stewart Wolf, did an experiment to find out — and came up with some amazing results.

He fed a group of human guinea pigs with clear consciences (they were told they were drinking in the interests of science) the same amount of grog as another group of ordinary drinkers were downing at a nearby pub. The aim of all of them was to get drunk — and, with the good professor footing the booze bill, they all did just that.

But, Dr Wolf reported later, not one of those who got smashed in the laboratory reported a hangover, while those who drank where they always drink woke up with throbbing heads, aching guts, horrible mouths etc.

So what does that prove, you may ask. Well, concluded Dr

Wolf, a hangover is nothing more than the showing of a person's guilt complex for getting drunk in the first place!

His theory is supported by other authorities. Explains Timothy Coffey, editor of the *Journal on Alcohol Studies*, "Come morning you are going to feel guilty about hanging one on. Guilt feelings about anything can give jitters and aches. So go ahead and concoct some foul-smelling remedy. It's a good way of punishing yourself and thereby relieving the guilt."

You'll be pleased to know you're not the only one suffering today. After extensive research, a Michigan University professor has now proved conclusively that pigs who drink too much suffer hangovers just like humans. He is now trying to discover the perfect hangover cure for pigs, which he claims should work on humans as well.

As proof, the professor cites humorist Henry Morton's saying: "One drink of wine, and you act like a monkey; two drinks and you strut like a peacock; three drinks and you roar like a lion; and four drinks — you behave like a pig."

7

No respectable drinker will agree with that — so in the pages that follow you'll find distinctly *human* hangover recipes developed over the ages and in many countries. There are so many, and their origins are often so obscure, that it has proved impossible in most cases to acknowledge the inventors. The **author and publisher can only say: "Thank you for your service to suffering humanity—we'll toast you all with our next drink!"**

How do you tell a stinking hangover from an ordinary hangover? If you feel so sick you're afraid you're going to die, you're suffering a pretty ordinary hangover. It's only a real stinker when you become terrified that you'll stay alive — to continue suffering.

————————

When I was two years of age she asked me not to drink, and then I made a resolution of total abstinence. That I have adhered to it and enjoyed the beneficent effects of it through all time, I owe by my grandmother. I have never drunk a drop from that day to this of any kind of water.

— MARK TWAIN

101 ways to cure that hangover

Mrs Theo. P. Winning's *Household Manual*, a medical bible for housewives last century, contains scores of old wives' remedies. To relieve a severe hangover headache, she advises, soak the feet in mustard and water until the headache vanishes.

Pepys' Breakfast Cure

Famous English diarist Samuel Pepys (pronounced "Peeps") had a boozy breakfast cure for hangovers, such as the one he served his suffering guests on New Year's morning 1661:

"A barrel of oysters, a dish of neats' tongues, a dish of anchovies, wine of all sorts and Northdowne Ale."

Cool, Baby, Cool!

Cut up an un-peeled cucumber into small pieces, then sprinkle with two teaspoons of salt. Drink several spoonfuls of the resulting liquid.

Pommy Hot Dog

Juice of two lemons
1 teaspoon mustard powder.
Mix the mustard with the lemon juice and drink in one hit.

Bushman's Corny Cure

An old Australian recipe from the makers of bush tucker:

Mix cornflower with buttermilk in a pot, then heat until almost boiling point. Season with salt and pepper to taste.

Royal Peter

Peter the Great of Russia swore that the only good hangover cure was warm brandy liberally spiced with pepper.

Bitter Bubbly

Pour ice-cold champagne into a chilled glass, add one teaspoon of cognac and a dash of angostura bitters, stir and drink.

Suffering Bastard

Attributed to a barman at Cairo's old Shepheard Hotel, this hangover cure calls for:

Brandy

Lime Juice

Gin

Take one-third of each. Add dash of bitters. Mix with ginger ale. Sip slowly.

Dying Bastard

As for Suffering Bastard, but add a shot of Bourbon.

Dead Bastard

As for Dying Bastard, but add a shot of rum.

Dairy Delight

One nip vodka

Two nips tomato juice

Slug of Worcestershire sauce

Two Alka-Seltzers
"A good squirt of cow's milk," preferably from the udder (full-cream milk from the milk bottle will do in an emergency).
Mix together, allowing the milk from the udder to foam up in the glass, or if from the bottle stir rapidly to get the same effect. Drink slowly.

Foaming Blood

Take a beer glass, fill it halfway with tomato juice, then top it up with beer.

Hot 'n Cold

Sitting with an ice-pack on your head and your feet in hot water "takes the blood from the brain", say some people, who claim it relieves the throbbing head and many other hangover symptoms.

Distilled Dynamite

In a whiskey tumbler, mix half a teaspoon of sugar with a dash of angostura bitters. Add 1.5 shots of rye whiskey and one ice cube. Fill the glass with chilled champagne, then add two dashes of absinthe. Drink.

Prairie Oyster

Drop a raw egg in a tumbler, season with salt and vinegar, Worcestershire or hot sauce. Then
Shut eyes, open mouth,
Murmur prayers for the soul,
Pop in and swallow whole...

Roman Bouncer

Roman drinkers believed prevention was better than cure —
so they regularly left the banquet hall to drink a glass or two of
sea water and be sick. Then they bounced back to the wine
and the party continued.

Tiger's Milk

(An authentic Thai hangover cure)

45ml of Baccardi
45ml of Cognac
Half cup of cream
Half cup of milk
Shake vigorously with ice, pour into a glass and flavor gently
with nutmeg.

Virgin Mary

Mix one can of tomato juice with half a cup of lemon juice,
salt and pepper and a celery stick. Drink.

Polish Bison

Attributed to author Kingsley Amis, this hangover cure requires you to mix a generous slug of vodka with a large teaspoon of Bovril beef extract, two tablespoons of lemon juice, water and pepper. Drink quickly.

Singapore Sling

To mix this favorite Oriental hangover cure, you need:

Juice of quarter lemon or 1 large lime
1 shot of cherry brandy
1.5 shots of gin
1 teaspoon sugar syrup
Dash of Angostura bitters.

Shake and strain into highball glass with one ice cube.
Fill glass with ginger ale.
Serve with slice of lemon peel.

Bloody Mary

Mix one part vodka with two to six parts tomato juice (the amount of tomato juice is determined by the ferocity of your hangover). Add dash of Worcestershire sauce. Serve with very thin slice of lemon floating on top.

Muscle Magic

Kingsley Amis offers this off-beat cure for hangovers:

"Upon awakening, if your wife or other partner is beside you, and (of course) willing, perform the sexual act as vigorously as you can. The exercise will do you good and you'll feel toned up emotionally."

Owl's That?

Pliny the Elder, a famous Roman, swore by Jupiter that the only morning-after cure was six raw owls' eggs swallowed in quick succession.

Swallow That!

In ancient Assyria, ground swallow beaks mixed with bitter myrrh was a prime recipe for a hangover.

Morning Glory Fizz

Juice of half a lime
Juice of half a lemon
1 egg white
2 teaspoons sugar syrup
1 pony of absinthe
1 jigger of Scotch

Shake together with crushed ice, strain into a large glass and top up with equal amount of soda water.

(From David Embury's *The Fine Art of Mixing Drinks*)

Cures Around The World

Norway: A glass of heavy cream to settle the rebellious stomach.

Switzerland: Brandy with a dash of peppermint.

Russia: Cucumber juice, heavily salted. In some parts they also eat black bread soaked in water for breakfast.

Germany: Sour herring with a beer chaser (or three). Sometimes the herring is combined with raw onions, sour cream or yogurt.

Puerto Rico: Rub half a lemon under your drinking arm.

Outer Mongolia: Pickled sheep's eye in tomato juice.
France: Thick black hot onion soup for breakfast.

Black Velvet

Pour half a Guinness into a glass, top up with an extra-dry champagne. Sip slowly. Repeat if necessary.

Extraordinary Bloody Mary

Attributed to Aussie chef extraordinaire Bernard King, it is made as follows:

Plug up your ears, then crush ice cubes in the blender. Half-fill a large glass with the crushed ice, packing tightly. Add a good slug of vodka, topped with tomato puree, dashes of celery salt, Tabasco sauce, garlic salt and celery seed. Stir briskly. Drink slowly. Remove the ear plugs and face the world.

Scots Guts

Two nips of whisky
One shot of Fernet Branca
Three dashes of Pernod
Pinch of salt

Dash of Tabasco.
Mix together. Stir gently. Add ice and strain into a tall glass.

Cayenne Fizz
Take a half-litre of champagne, sprinkle with cayenne pepper, drink slowly.

Glorious Morning
This hangover cure consists of a measure of Fernet Branca and a dash of peppermint. Swallow very fast.

A Vitamin, I See
Vitamin C can not only cure hangover, it can also sober up a dead drunk, an Australian doctor has found.

He says large doses (between five and 30gm) of vitamin C, taken very quickly, makes a hangover disappear. And it does not matter whether you take the tablets before or after you drink.

"Results are very dramatic," he reports. "Patients come in drunk with very high blood alcohol levels. Some are noisy, aggressive and hard to deal with. Others are dead drunk and unconscious or having fits.

"I give them 30gm of vitamin C in a solution intravenously, slowly over 10 or 20 minutes. Within minutes the fits stop, they sober up, lose their belligerence and become easier to handle. Some fall into a deep sleep lasting up to three hours and then wake up feeling normal."

His treatment has the support of Nobel Prize-winner Dr. Linus Pauling, who agrees a massive dose of vitamin C is the best way to cure a hangover.

Slippery Slime

In the Middle Ages, a popular hangover remedy was a mixture of bitter almonds and raw eel.

The Jules Reviver

This hair-of-the-dog hangover cure comes from the famous Jules Bar in Jermyn Street, London:

Pimms No 1 with a dash of Grand Marnier, topped with chilled champagne.

Heart Starter

A double Gin, mixed with water and liver salts, then gulped down quickly for maximum effect.

Dr Twinkle's Hangover Tonic

2-3 pieces of cucumber
Few sprigs of parsley
Stick of celery
Lemon rind
2 grapes

3 tablespoons sugar
Dash vanilla essence.
Liquidize, then pour into the first glass. This is the main
drink. Next, mix together:
Half cup of milk
1 teaspoon Creme de Cacao
3 tablespoons cream
Pinch of salt
1 teaspoon sugar
Dash of bitters
1 teaspoon wheat germ.
Beat in two eggs, then pour into the second glass.
Drink contents of glass one, followed quickly by the contents
of glass two.

Expense Account Cures

Hangover cures collected by the US financial newspaper *The
Wall Street Journal*, for readers who know all about expense
account drinking:
A huge slug of bitters in a cold beer.

A few whiffs of pure oxygen.
Buttermilk heavily spiced with salt and pepper.
Chewing wild lettuce leaves.
A cup of plain yogurt.
A cup of cherry-leaf tea (no milk or sugar).

Tart Eggs
Mix together vinegar and raw eggs — then gulp down in one hit.

Brown Bubbly
French wine producers met with a mixed response when they invited more than 200 doctors to a wine cellar — to try out a champagne-and-cognac hangover cure.

The mixture of one part cognac to three parts of champagne was pronounced "not a bad drop" by members of the Physicians Wine Appreciation Society of New York. But not one medic was willing to hail it as the perfect hangover remedy.

Royal Prunier
Said to be the Queen's favorite hangover cure, this remedy consists of four ounces of champagne mixed with four ounces of orange juice over ice.

Wooster Booster
Put a raw egg, yolk unbroken, into a cup with liberal quantities of Worcestershire sauce. For speedy relief, gulp the mixture in one go, making sure the egg does not break until it reaches the back of your throat. That is claimed to take away the nausea.

Brandy Branca

Attributed to wine expert Len Evans, this hangover cure tastes horrible but is said to work wonders:

One ounce of brandy
Dash of Fernet Branca
Mix together and drink.

Hangover Casserole

To make this nasty concoction, reports Clement Freud, you:
Slice very thinly half a kilo of onions, simmer in 250gm (half a pound) of butter until soft, then pour a bottle of champagne into the pan. Decant the mixture in a soup tureen, cover with a layer of Camembert cheese and sprinkle toasted breadcrumbs on top. Bake in a medium oven until the cheese melts and the crumbs have been crisped.
Eat for breakfast after seasoning with black pepper.

Herring delight

12 salted herrings
250ml cider vinegar
3 Juniper berries
cloves
peppercorns
a dash of water.
Blend together:
Drink slowly for breakfast.

007's Licence to Cure

James Bond (in *Thunderball* and *Moonraker*) uses this hangover cure:

Two aspirin taken with a glass of fruit salts — and plenty of pretty women on whom to feast those bloodshot eyes until they recover their usual lustful sparkle.

Highland Honey

Take one ounce of Scotch, one ounce of cream, and half an ounce of honey. Shake heavily in a cocktail shaker and add to shaved ice in a cocktail glass. Drink immediately.

"I say, old chap..."

A British doctor claims the best hangover cure is a tall glass of lemon juice and fructose mixed together.

Hart's Cure

Patented by Englishman Nathan Hart in 1904, this cure for everything from hangovers to consumption is easy to make — but not that easy to swallow. You mix two garlic bulbs with a bottle of prime brandy, then warm the mixture slowly for a week before drinking.

Dry Gunpowder

One-third dry vermouth
One third Pernod
One-third brandy.
Stir well and serve.

You are what you eat

Eating before going out on a junket helps you drink more before you get drunk because it slows down the rate at which the stomach absorbs alcohol. Some people also claim going on

a binge on a full stomach reduces the agony of the hangover that follows. A pre-drinking meal recommended by one doctor who is regarded as a world authority on hangovers:

Eat a bowl of milk and cornflakes (packed with vitamin B) and an orange or two (for its vitamin C), followed by a plate of potatoes, well salted and mashed with butter.

Some doctors say eating a breakfast of milk and steak is just the thing for hangover belly aches and nausea, with a couple of aspirin to settle the headache.

The Scots swear that hot porridge for breakfast is the best treatment for a hangover, particularly one induced by scotch.

Bees' Knees

8 parts gin
1 part honey
2 parts lemon juice
Shake with cracked ice. Strain and add two parts of orange juice. Drink.

22

Egg Burp

Pour half a bottle of beer into a short glass. Mix in one raw egg, stir until foam subsides.

Apple Banger

1 shot apple brandy
1 shot Dubonnet
Dash Angostura bitters.
Stir well with ice, strain into glass.

Pony Express

1 shot brandy
2 shots of port
Quarter teaspoon sugar
1 egg yolk
Stir and drink gently.

Brandy Pick-Up

2 shots brandy
White of 1 egg
Freshly squeezed juice of 1 lemon
Teaspoon castor sugar.
Shake well, strain into tall glass, fill with soda water.

STOP! COMPULSORY DRINK BREAK!
It's time to have a drink and find out if you're
sober enough to continue reading the hangover
cures. Check the eye-chart on the following
pages– if you pass the test, turn to Page 26.

HOW SOZZL

YOU
READ
THEN YOU
ABSOLUTELY, POS

D ARE YOU?

F

CAN'T

THIS

MUST BEE

IVE PLE-EYED!

Captain Blood

4 shots Bundaberg rum
1 shot lime juice
2 dashes bitters.
Stir quickly and serve neat or over ice if preferred.

Pepper Pow-Wow!

1 shot Scotch Whisky
Juice of half a lemon
1 teaspoon Worcestershire sauce
1 teaspoon chili sauce.
1 dash Tabasco sauce
3 dashes bitters.
Stir well.

Swiss Belly Blaster

1 part Vermouth
2 parts absinthe
Half teaspoon sugar syrup
1 egg white.
Shake well with ice.
Pour into tall glass (with the ice) and top up with soda water.

Water Torture

Before going to bed, drink half a litre of lightly salted water
and two aspirin. Continue drinking the lightly-salted water
every time you wake up during the night to restore the fluid
balance. Alcohol dehydrates the body and many experts
believe this is a major cause of hangovers.

Sugar 'n Spice

Sugary soft drinks with plenty of fizz for breakfast is regarded as an excellent hangover cure by many sufferers. To turn in into a true "hair-of-the-dog", add a shot of rum or brandy.

Cliffhanger

Favorite of the fictional private eye Cliff Hardy, this cure consists of cask white wine diluted with soda water. Increase the concentration of the wine until the hangover vanishes.

Green Gratitude

Pour a generous jigger of creme de menthe into a tall glass, then top off with soda water.

Jamaican Eyeball Plucker

1 shot overproof rum
1 teaspoon cream
1 teaspoon honey.
Shake well with ice. Strain into glass.

Spiced Soda

Pour warmed-up soda water into a tall glass.
Add liberal dash of bitters.
Drink as fast as possible.

Foaming brekky

Many serious drinkers, particularly in Australia and Germany, believe implicitly that the best morning-after cure is a few glasses of beer for breakfast. For speedier relief—
and if your stomach can handle it—add angostura bitters to

the beer. Others say flat beer is even better, so leave a can or two open before going to bed.

Blood 'n Guts
Flagellation to draw plenty of blood was the ancient Greek way to cure a hangover — when anyone was bold enough to admit having one, that is!

Stone the crows ... er, hangovers
Ancient Greeks believed amethyst would protect them against hangovers, so they placed the precious stones in the bottom of their drinking vessels or imbedded them in the side of their goblets.

Food for thought
Through the ages, many self-proclaimed hangover experts have advocated chewing your way to health and happiness. Here are some of their suggestions.

Slowly chew raw root ginger.

Hot bacon rolls dripping with fat.

"Greasy spoon" hamburger with lashings of ketchup, washed down with tomato juice.

Sauerkraut and juicy sausages.

Chinese spring rolls.

Grapefruit.

Dry toast.

A cabbage a day...

Keeping sober while drinking great quantities of wine — and avoiding a hangover — was a problem for the old Egyptians — until they discovered boiled cabbage!

A visitor to Egypt reported that "they are the only people amongst whom it is a custom at their feasts to eat boiled cabbages before all the rest of their foods — and even to this very time they do so, and many people add cabbage seeds to potions which they prepare as preventives against drunkenness and suffering the next day".

Cabbages also helped prevent hangovers, the old Romans believed — so much so they wrote a poem about it's restorative values:

Last evening you were drinking deep,
So now your head aches. Go to sleep:
Take some boiled cabbage when you wake,
And there's an end to your headache!

(Quoted in *A Toast: Your Health!* by D.L. Ziegler.)

Dr Jones' Honey Humdinger

Immediately after waking, force down six teaspoonfuls of

honey every 20 minutes for the first hour. After three hours, repeat the treatment, then eat a soft-boiled egg.

Jumping Jackrabbit

This old Wild West cure, from the days when bad whiskey was served in tough saloons, treated many a gun-slinger's hangover. It's a treatment for those who suffer hangovers often enough to take precautions well in advance.

The recipe calls for "plenty of droppings from a jackrabbit", which should be well dried. You mix the dried dung into a strong tea with hot water, strain and drink every 30 minutes.

Bushies Delight

Australian boozers seeking a cure last century were given the following advice: "Put half an ounce of ground quassia into one pint of good strong vinegar. Let it stand for 24 hours, then bottle, and every time a hangover strikes take two teaspoonfuls in a little water and drink it down. The pain will gradually leave, but have it close at hand so there need be no excuse to suffer so much from the whisky again."

Make Up Your Mind!

The tranquilizer Librium cures hangovers and sobers up drinkers twice as fast as coffee, a Swedish scientist told the 28th International Congress on alcohol and alcoholism.

Dr Leonard Goldberg tested more than 1000 pie-eyed volunteers to reach that conclusion.

But before you rush off to your friendly doctor for a Librium prescription, here's the bad news. A Sydney University research team has reported that the effects of alcohol were con-

siderably increased if the drinker was taking either Librium or another tranquilizer, Valium.

Voodoo Corker

In Haiti, voodoo extends even to hangovers. An instant cure is produced, say locals, when you stick 13 black-headed pins in the cork of the bottle that gave you the hangover.

Grey Guts

Chimney-sweeps last century swore by this hangover cure: Warm a cup of milk, then gently mix in a level teaspoonful of fine soot (soot created by burning hardwood is the best). Drink slowly. Repeat after 30 minutes if you are still feeling a bit off.

Adriatic Boot

Baume de Floriani, a mixture of Chianti, turpentine and a wide range of spices, was a popular hangover cure in Italy last century.

31

Bitter and Twisted

Two shots of good-quality cider vinegar — not cider — is a favorite way to cure hangovers in the west of England. And no wonder — they have lots of apple trees there and make cider for much of the country.

On the Trot

One popular cure for hangovers in the Low Counties of Holland is a trotter-and-liver soup. You boil sheep's trotters, cow's livers and oatmeal for six hours, then strain and eat the soup while hot.

Devil's Delight

Take one cup of milk, mix in two tablespoons of castor oil, and warm the mixture until lukewarm. Season with red cayenne pepper. Sip slowly while still warm.

Toasted Red Indian

Burnt toast soaked in milk, then eaten with a spoon like porridge, is said to work wonders on a hangover, particularly one caused by red wine.

Mark Elder's Pedestrian Cure

Hangover veteran Mark Elder (who designed this book) offers the following advice:

"Lots of oxygen and greasy food work wonders in fighting hangovers. So, instead of taking a cab home from the pub, walk at least part of the way — and use the money you save to buy the greasiest hamburger with 'the works' to keep you company. It works every time." There is one qualification

— you need to be sober enough to find your way home!

Kamikaze Cure?

The Japanese cure a hangover by wearing a gauze surgical mask soaked in saki.

Genghis Khan's Cure

1 teaspoon Epsom salts
1 teaspoon cream of tartar
1 teaspoon ground ginger.
Mix together, then dissolve one or more teaspoons in a glass of water and drink.

Let it all hang out!

If all else fails and spewing is the only solution, you can make a very fast acting emetic by mixing mustard powder with water.

Alcohol is the anaesthesia by which we endure the operation of life.
— GEORGE BERNARD SHAW

What's behind a hangover?

"Water is best," Pindar, a Greek poet and wowser, said piously 2500 years ago. Of course, we all know that's not true, but we also have to admit that water does not make you drunk or give you a hangover. So what is a hangover? There are almost as many theories as there are medical scientists, but generally they agree it's a combination of several of the following:

✔ Too little fluid in the body, or dehydration.

✔ Too much fluid in the brain.

✔ A chemical created by alcohol that produces side effects.

✔ Too much lactic acid in the stomach.

✔ Too much carbon dioxide in the blood.

What causes the terrible suffering?

As a rule of thumb, the darker the drink, the worse the hangover. Thus you'll do best to drink white spirits and still white wines, rather than nipping into the brandy, sherry, red wine, or dark rum. Sparkling wines of any color, such as champagne, have more acids, which also increase the severity of a hangover. They also make you drunk more quickly, because the bubbles help the body to absorb the alcohol at an increased rate.

It's the alcohol in the booze that makes you drunk, but that's absorbed by the body pretty quickly. The main cause of a hang-

over is not alcohol as such, but dirty little demons called *congeners* (impurities) that lurk inside every kind of booze. Congeners are mostly chemical by-products of fermentation and maturing processes and give the distinctive flavor and characteristics to "natural" wines, spirits and beers. More than 100 congeners have so far been identified.

The amount of impurities in various drinks should warn you how lethal the hangovers they cause are likely to be.

One scientific way to check this theory is to partake of sufficient quantities of various drinks — a different one each night — to give you a hangover. You can then compare the ferocity of the headache, nausea and so on of each. Or you can simply refer to the following *HANGOVER SEVERITY CHART,* which is based on scientific research and hard-earned human experience through the ages.

35

HOW TO PICK YOU[R]

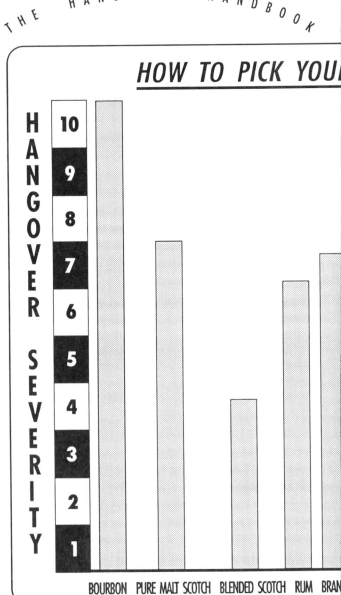

MORNING-AFTER PAIN

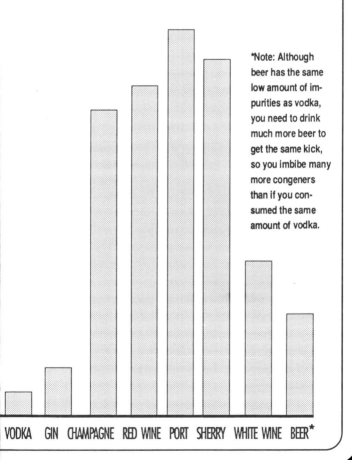

*Note: Although beer has the same low amount of impurities as vodka, you need to drink much more beer to get the same kick, so you imbibe many more congeners than if you consumed the same amount of vodka.

VODKA GIN CHAMPAGNE RED WINE PORT SHERRY WHITE WINE BEER*

Great drunks of history

No one will ever know who discovered booze, but there can be no doubt that there were drunks from the moment someone sampled that very first drink. And since then, humanity has been guzzling down the good stuff in huge quantities. Here are a few lurid tales of those who drank themselves into the history books.

Sailing on a sea of booze

Admiral Edward Russell, commander of the British Mediterranean Fleet, had a truly stupendous appetite for booze — even for a sailor in the hard-drinking 17th Century.

After trying — and almost succeeding — to drink dry all of Spain, he threw his booziest party starting on 26 November 1694 at his sumptuous headquarters in the Spanish town of Alicante.

A group of government officials from London were visiting, and to impress them, the red-nosed Admiral turned the entire outdoor fountain in the garden into a huge punch bowl!

It was so big that a row-boat could float around it, manned by a young sailor who served up punch for the thirsty guests. But the fumes were so potent that the sailor had to be replaced every 15 minutes to prevent him from passing out.

The party went on for an entire week, with a silk canopy going up when it started to rain to prevent the punch from being diluted. The Admiral and his guests — more than 6000 attended during the course of the week — drank and drank each day till they passed out, then started again next morning. The party ended only when the rowboat ran aground for lack of punch.

If you reckon you'd like to re-create the good Admiral's hospitality (and your pocket can stand it), here's the recipe for his gigantic punch:

Four hogsheads (1150 litres/254 gallons) of brandy
1135 litres/249 gallons of Malaga wine
90 litres/19.8 gallons of lime juice
591kg/1300lb of brown sugar
2500 lemons
2kg/4.4lb of grated nutmeg
500 litres of water.

Cut the lemons into quarters and mix all the ingredients together in one outdoor fountain or small pool, using the oars of a boat to stir until all the ingredients are dissolved. Drink with several thousand friends.

My kingdom (and my wife!) for a bottle

George IV (nicknamed Prinny) was England's most drunken and fattest king ever — and not without reason. Even when suffering from an inflamed bladder, rheumatism and gout, his *breakfast* would consist of three beefsteaks and two pigeons, washed down with a bottle of wine, half a bottle of champagne, two glasses of port and "several" glasses of brandy.

It is claimed his wife drove Prinny to drink when he was still the Prince of Wales. He first met his foul-smelling bride, Caroline of Brunswick, three days before their wedding and discovered she had not yet adopted the English custom of washing and changing her clothes at least once a week. Prinny was so revolted by her smell that he hurriedly kissed her, then went to a corner of the room and started drinking brandy — and never completely sobered up again. Prinny was still in his cups on their wedding day in April 1795, spending the night in a drunken stupor on the floor of the royal bedroom.

So much did Prinny despise his wife that, at their coronation on 19 July 1821, he ordered guards to lock the doors to prevent her getting in. Of course, the good king, who by now weighed more than 238 pounds, was again almost blotto, so he had to be supported into Westminster Abbey by eight noblemen. At the reception that followed, he drank bottle after bottle of brandy. The Royal physician was on standby and each time the king passed out he was bled until he revived— only to continue drinking and eating.

Stinking Caroline certainly had enough vices to drive any man to drink. Even before she married her Royal cousin, she shocked the crowned heads of Europe by turning up topless at a society ball in Geneva, dipping her nipples into the champagne glasses to cool down. On another occasion she joined a hunting party wearing only a pumpkin on her head, explaining that "nothing is so cool or so comfortable".

Welsh shall we have another?

Welsh poet Dylan Thomas boasted that he was "the most drunken man in the world" and once travelled to America as part of his "insatiable quest for naked women in wet mackintoshes."·Born on October 27, 1914, he said he was driven to drink by the Tax Collector, who snatched all his earnings

before he even received them after he fell behind with his tax payments for a few years. Whatever the reason, he certainly drank more than he ever paid in taxes.

He particularly loved American and Canadian whiskeys and became so inspiring when drunk that many rich people vied with one another to buy him drinks.

Even at work at the staid BBC, where booze was banned, Thomas managed to keep himself going by sipping from a bottle marked "champagne wine tonic", ostensibly for his health. He was on air one morning when he suddenly drained the bottle, stopped talking for a moment, then remarked: "Somebody's boring me — I think it's me!" Then he walked off in search of another drink.

Thomas was only 39 when, one November night in New York, he set out on a final drinking binge — shortly after his doctors had told him to give up drink altogether. Before he collapsed, he said proudly: "I've had 18 straight whiskeys. I think that's a record." He died in St Vincent's Hospital, New York, where the cause of death was given as "an acute alcoholic insult to the brain".

Another Welshman, Dr Clive Arkle, was so drunk so often that police took away his firearms licence because of his "intemperate habits and lack of competitive activity". The doctor went to court to prove them wrong. He testified that his regular *daily drop of 30 pints of bitter* was only enough to "tighten up the eyeballs" — and produced a mass of trophies which he had won after one such visit to the pub. His appeal, strangely enough, was disallowed.

Dr Arkle took an oath on the Bible and then testified with his hands hanging by his sides, so the magistrate was probably suspicious about his testimony. The reason for this is simple: the English word testimony has a very unusual origin. When ancient Romans, drunk or sober, swore an oath to tell the truth, they solemnly placed their right hand on their testicles and only then were they allowed to testify. Whether about tightening eyeballs or anything else...

Noah your drinks and you'll live longer

The joy of a booze-up and the agony of a hangover began with Noah, or so the Bible tells us. For, as we read in Genesis, "Noah, the tiller of the soil, was the first (man in the world) to plant a vineyard. And he drank of the wine and became drunk."

Drunk as a skunk, in fact, for he passed out stark naked in his tent!

But a good session with the bottle (or was it a leather cask in those days?) certainly did Noah no harm. He not only survived

being seasick on the Ark, but lived to the ripe old age of 950!

Here's to you and your ghost!

When Philip the Handsome of Spain died almost 500 years ago, having drunk himself to death, his wife Joanna took to drink — and never again became sober enough to leave their marital bed.

For company, she kept Philip's corpse in bed next to her for three years, drinking toasts to his health every morning and evening. Her subjects named her Joanna the Mad.

The smells from the corpse (no longer handsome) finally forced the servants to remove it after Joanna passed out one day — and she continued toasting it, never even knowing it had gone!

In Like Flynn (and Niven) at Cirrhosis-by-the-Sea

Errol Flynn and David Niven shared a house in Hollywood which they aptly named "Cirrhosis-by-the-Sea". For a while the two dabbled with other drugs as well, until they settled down and concentrated on booze. Flynn later admitted he had tried everything from mainlining heroin to putting a pinch of cocaine on his penis—as an aphrodisiac.

When he was drunk — and that was often — Tasmanian-born Flynn loved nothing better than a good old barroom brawl, which he usually won.

The two almost succeeded in drinking Hollywood dry, and in the process established an amazing reputation for wenching and wild behavior. As Sheridan Morley recounts in his biography of Niven, *The Other Side of the Moon*, "Flynn and Niven were a couple of the likeliest lads around town. Female stars were extra-maritally bedded, films made, bars were

broken up; it was a case of 'no job too big to too small'...
David was able to revert to the teenage tearaway who had
smuggled a prostitute into his public school." Among these
drunken exploits was smuggling Joan Bennett into Flynn's
bedroom at Cirrhosis-by-the-Sea under the nose of her under-
standably aggrieved husband Walter Wanger — who later shot
another man in the testicles for merely making a pass at Joan!

Lusty Pope lived for wine, women and song

Early Popes featured prominently among the great drunks of
history. Pope John XII was a prime example. Born in Rome
around 837, he was only 18 when he took over the Holy See —
and introduced one of the most drunken and depraved reigns
in Catholic history which earned him the nickname "The
Christian Caligula".

He threw constant parties at which female pilgrims were not
only raped and man-handled, but also sent to work as pros-
titutes in the Lateran Palace. His palace guard was a gang of
cut-throats who robbed and terrorized the city as they sought
new virgins for the Pope to enjoy.

Almost never sober — when he was, he suffered from a terrible hangover — the Pope once ordained a bishop in a stable
and took great pleasure from watching priests who had
angered him being mutilated.

He died at the age of 27 — very drunk and in the arms of his
mistress.

To mix a *Pope*, you need:

Tokay (a rich, sweet and aromatic Hungarian wine)
Ripe bitter oranges
Sugar

Nutmeg and cloves
Pour the wine, hot or cold, over the oranges, mix in sugar and spices to taste.

To mix a *Cardinal*, use red wine such as claret or burgundy, instead of Tokay; for a *Bishop*, substitute white instead of red wine.

Drunk and disorderly! Who, me?

Arthur Mason takes the title as arguably the greatest British drunk of modern times. After being convicted in 1978 for the 59th time of being drunk and disorderly, the magistrate informed the amiable drunk that no publican in his native Basingstoke would ever be allowed to serve him again.

In fact, the court ruled, they would be guilty of an offence if they did. But Arthur was too drunk to understand — so the magistrate had to wait until the next day when he had sobered up to inform him of the ban. When the sentence finally sank in, Arthur found a way to outwit the law — he moved to the next town!

Song of the Vodka Boatmen

Is the Russian town of Krasnensk, in Byelorussia, home to the biggest boozers in the world? Judge for yourself. The town has a population of only 6000, yet consumes 150,000 bottles of vodka a month — an average of 25 bottles per person, including children!

French General Bisson, one of Napoleon's right-hand men who was involved in the invasion of Russia, drank eight bottles of wine every day — *with breakfast!*

The sweetest way to die?

Grieved by the death of his favorite brother-in-law, the drunken old Anglo-Saxon King Hundung decided to drown his sorrows — literally! He called all his noblemen together for a feast and had a huge vat of mead (wine made from honey) placed in the center of the hall. When his guests had drunk their fill and were about to pass out, the good king threw himself into the vat and drowned.

Another drunken king also used wine to kill — but this time the victim was not himself. England's King Edward IV forced his brother George, Duke of Clarence, to drink himself to death — literally. He had George put to death in the Tower of London in 1478 by drowning him in a tub of sweet Malmsey wine — because he felt threatened by George's sober habits.

Other famous people also died strangely. Aeschylus, father of Greek drama, was killed in 456 BC by a tortoise dropped on his bald head by an eagle! The bird, keen to break the shell, had apparently mistaken the shiny dome for a stone. Experimenting with refrigeration, the philosopher Francis Bacon was stuffing a chicken with snow in 1626 when he caught a cold — which killed him.

'I bet you don't know this...'

? How would you like to stand in the pub all night and win round after round of free drinks? You are in luck! By reading *The Hangover Handbook*, you can make that dream come true—and amuse your drinking buddies at the same time.

The following 20 questions should be worth a round of drinks each - unless of course someone else in the bar has been wise enough to buy a copy of *The Hangover Handbook* as well! All the answers appear in the book, but in case you want to quiz your buddies before you've read it all, the answers are on page 62.

1. Name the famous poet who called himself "the most drunken man in the world" and lusted after "naked women in wet mackintoshes"?

2. Where is Australia's narrowest pub?

3. How do James Bond, the Japanese and voodoo priests cure hangovers?

4. Which two famous drinkers named their home *Cirrhosis-by-the-Sea?*

5. What is a teetotaller?

6. Which idiots first taxed booze?

7. How do you say "Hangover" in German and "Cheers" in Welsh?

8. What are the impurities called that scientists blame for hangovers?

9. How did lusty King Henry VIII punish palace staff who made female servants pregnant?

10. What distance does alcohol travel through your bloodstream before your entire body is pickled?

11. Which famous boozer said: "A woman drove me to drink — and I never even wrote to thank her"?

12. In which country is wine called "the milk of the elderly"?

13. How do you make *Scots Guts* and *Highland Honey*?

14. Why is St Brigid of Ireland loved by drinkers and disliked by brewers?

15. Who advocated the following hangover cure: "A barrel of oysters, a dish of neats' tongues, a dish of anchovies, wine of all sorts and Northdowne Ale"?

16. Why did the wines of ancient Egypt and ancient Libya keep drinkers running to the loo?

17. How do you mix an alcoholic Pope, an alcoholic Cardinal and an alcoholic Bishop outside the Catholic Church?

18. Which Australian State or Territory boasts the largest beer consumption in the world — 236.4 litres a year for every man, woman and child?

19. Who was Mr Grog?

20. Which right Royal tippler believed that the only hangover cure was warm brandy liberally spiced with pepper?

The pub survivor's guide

Mixing drinks does not make you drunk – it's the alcohol in each drink that's the culprit. But starting the night with beer and then switching to spirits can make you drunk more quickly than you'd imagine. The reason is simple: your palate gets dulled by the beer and can't appreciate the strength of the spirits.

So you toss them down at the same rate as the beer, consuming a lot more alcohol than you think you are.

Don't say you haven't been warned!

Coffee? No thanks!

Strong coffee is no antidote for booze. It can actually make matters worse, according to a Sydney University research team.

They found that caffeine produced "a wide-awake drunk who could be more dangerous because if he had not taken the coffee he would have been more aware of the impairment of his other faculties."

Get tanked up in style

The world's largest pewter beer tankard, made in Malaysia in 1985, can hold 2796 litres/614 gallons, enough to give several hundred people a giant hangover!

At this clinic, the cure ends with a cuppa!

The world's first hangover clinic, which opened in London in 1971, offered sufferers the following treatment:

First you have a sauna to sweat out the last of the alcohol still lurking in your bloodstream. This is followed by a fruit-sugar preparation laced with vitamins B1, B6, C and garden mint. Next you are given a few gulps of pure oxygen. Then, to help your screaming intestines absorb all that goodness, you get a "gentle and sympathetic massage", a spirit alcohol rub and, as a grand finale and tribute to the virtues of teetotalism, a nice strong cuppa tea.

Boasted Managing Director Connor Walsh: "You go out fresh as a two-year-old!"

What a way for a drink to go!

The human body has 206 bones and 96,000 kilometres

(51,651 miles) of blood vessels, some so thin that blood corpuscles can only pass through in single file.

Impurities in booze chasing through those thin veins cause the throbbing ache and sick feeling we call a hangover.

What to do when the dog bites

Why do people refer to the morning-after drink that cures a hangover as "a hair of the dog that bit you"?

In the days when superstition and medical science were one, it was believed that the bite from a mad dog could be cured by putting some of its hairs on the wound. The first reference to the term in English occurred in 1546.

Why love is like a cocktail party

The energy expended by humans in a single act of lovemaking is the same as that needed to stand at cocktail parties and make small talk for about eight hours.

And while on the subject of mating games: Cobras take between two minutes and 24 hours to mate, while snails can keep at it for up to 12 hours. Impala often make love on the run.

How Randy King Henry saved beer money

King Henry VIII, whose lust for female flesh led to the founding of the Church of England, insisted that his male staff should be punished if they indulged in extra-marital sex.

The regulations for his Officers of the Bedchamber stated: "Such pages as cause the maids of the King's household to become mothers will go without beer for a month."

Miracle of the bathtub

Perhaps the most welcome miracle performed by a Catholic Saint was when St Brigid of Ireland changed her bath water into beer for thirsty visitors to her Kildare abbey in the 1500s.

The refreshed band of drinkers reported afterwards that the beer had a "saintlike" quality and taste.

And while on the subject of bizarre stories about saints: Pontius Pilate has been canonized as a Saint in the Ethiopian Church.

Nelson's blood!

After the battle of Trafalgar, Admiral Lord Nelson was shipped back to England in a cask of brandy, so that his body would be fresh for the State funeral. When the body was removed, the brandy was given to sailors so they could drink a toast to their departed commander — which they happily did.

Give love the boozer's boot
Egyptians believed you could cure love-sickness by drinking beer out of an old shoe.

Blasted booze!
Most people who indulge in a tipple know that spirits are a certain percentage proof, which indicates the relative quantities of water and alcohol in the mixture. Scientifically, proof spirit has a specific gravity of 12 over 13 at 51 degrees F. The original proof test employed a more practical kind of science: spirit poured over gunpowder and lit would eventually fire the powder if it was proof; if under-proof, the water remaining after the alcohol had burned off would prevent the powder from igniting.

Heidi's brew packs a punch
The world's most potent beer is brewed in Switzerland. Samichlaus Bier has 13.7 percent alcohol.

54

That's only part of the story...

The Northern Territory of Australia boasts the largest beer consumption in the world — 236.4 litres a year for every man, woman and child. Which means some men must drink a lot more than that!

Brown champagne by Royal command

Frederick the Great of Prussia loved drinking coffee — but only if it was made with champagne. It is not known what cure he used for champagne-coffee hangovers.

No room for beer bellies

Australia's smallest pub can be seen in the heart of Kalgoorlie, where it did brisk business between 1899 and 1924. A mere 3.35 metres wide, the British Arms was strategically placed opposite the busy Hannan Street railway station, which meant it quenched the thirst of miners both coming to and leaving the fabulously rich Western Australian goldfield. Today it is the Gold Mile Museum, which holds many fascinating goldrush relics.

To drink, or not to drink...

In Manitoba, Canada, local law prohibits drinking beer in the loo. And in the Canadian province of Saskatchewan, it is illegal to drink water in a beer parlor.

Monk(ey) business in Olde England

John, King of England from 1199 to 1216, liked a new kind of beer prepared in his honor so much that he drank himself to death on it! But, in an attempt to convince St Peter their king was not a drunk but a holy man, his loyal subjects dressed him in a monk's outfit for his burial.

Plastered on a penny!

The phrase *beer money* goes back almost 200 years. English soldiers traditionally received a ration of beer each day, the equivalent of the naval nip of rum or grog (watered down rum). Between 1800 and 1823 they were given an allowance of a penny a day beer money instead, which eventually became synonymous with money to be spent on pleasure.

Dutch courage

A former Dutch military custom of drinking spirits, particularly gin, before going into battle is the most likely origin of the derogatory idiom *Dutch courage*.

What bad word starts with a T?

That horrible word *teetotal* was invented by a New York temperance society which demanded that new members put a huge "T" next to their names whenever they signed them to signify Total abstinence from booze.

They soon became known as T-totals and gave the English language the word *teetotal*.

The five reasons for drinking

Good wine, a friend, or being dry,
Or lest we should be by and by,
or any other reason why...

— 16TH CENTURY SAYING

The taxman always taketh

The first known tax on booze was introduced in 3400 BC in the ancient Egyptian city of Memphis, on the Nile.

The tax was charged on barley wine, which, strange as it may sound, was actually the first known form of beer.

Grog has a human face

When you go on the grog, you're actually drinking to the memory of Admiral Edward Vernon, who got the nickname "Old Grog" because he wore a cloak of coarse cloth called grogram.

He was labeled a cheapskate when, in 1740, he declared that Royal Navy sailors could no longer have their neat half-pint of rum, but that it should be diluted with water. This mixture immediately became known as grog. And, with his sailors no longer pie-eyed by noon, Old Grog actually won some naval battles. So the Navy decided grog was a good thing — and henceforth it was the only drink issued to sailors.

The daily grog ration was abolished in 1970.

Mother's milk!

The weekly children's food ration in a British hospital in 1632 included two gallons of beer.

First drops Down Under

Australia's first brewery was started by John Boston, who used maize and the leaves and stalks of the Cape gooseberry to brew beer in 1796 in Sydney. The first government brewery was opened in Parramatta in 1804.

Holy XXX!

In the Middle Ages, beer did not include hops and was not preserved, so you drank it as you made it — and that kept the monks who were the main brewers in Merrie Olde England very merry indeed!

It was the monks who first put crosses — later to become the signs "XX" and "XXX" — on beer barrels to indicate that the beer inside had been brewed in the monastery and was of guaranteed quality.

What a weird Libyan libation

The Libyans, 2400 years ago, had a weird way to prevent hangovers after their mammoth wine drinking orgies: they mixed their wine with sea water! This made them so sick they never got really drunk enough to suffer. The historian Strabo says they spent much of the feast time in the loo.

These fellahs know their booze

What is booze? Strictly speaking, it's a potent beer-like brew made from barley by the good fellahs of Egypt.

To make *Boozah*, as they call it, they place barley in an earthenware vessel which is buried in the ground. When the barley starts to germinate, it is crushed, made into a dough and baked until a crust forms. The crust is dried and carried around the desert with the fellahs in the form of a cake.

When they reach an oasis, instead of drinking the water, they use it to dissolve this cake of dehydrated beer, which immediately starts to ferment.

Within hours they have enough boozah to make them very merry — and provide a "hair of the dog" in the morning.

Western travellers who sampled the brew wrote about it in English and the name was soon applied to all kinds of alcoholic drinks — and to the boozers who enjoy them.

Egyptian wines, reported the Roman historian Pliny around the time of Christ, were "remarkable for their sweetness and laxative qualities".

He wrote: "Wines which are more carefully mixed with sea water do not cause headache. They loosen the bowels, excite the stomach, cause inflation and assist digestion".

In France, wine is known as "the milk of the elderly".

Steamy tale of beer and brewers

The first steam engine used in a brewery is still in existence — and can be seen at the Powerhouse Museum in Sydney. Built by Boulton and Watt of Birmingham, the steam engine was first used in the Whitbread brewery in England in 1785 and shipped to Australia 102 years later.

Pie-eyed for love!

Having a sweetheart with a long name could easily turn you into a drunk in Roman times. When toasting her, tradition demanded that you drink a cup of wine for each letter in her name.

Thirsty Sandgropers

Australia's only hangover study, carried out a few years ago, showed Western Australia leading the field, with 38 percent of those polled suffering at least one hangover during the short survey period. New South Wales came second with 28 percent, followed by SA, Victoria, Tasmania and Queensland.

... And thirstier Scots

In 1842 the Scots — men, women and children together — drank a staggering 5,595,186 gallons of whisky, equal to more than 2 gallons each. American whiskey is called Bourbon because it was first made in Bourbon County, Kentucky, in 1789.

St Patrick not only chased all the snakes from Ireland, but tradition has it that he also introduced the then barbaric Irish tribes to the fine art of distilling Irish Whisky. Apparently the holy man liked a tipple or two himself!

Do you smell a rat?

The custom of embracing women by their friends and relatives was introduced, reports Joseph Haydn in his *Dictionary of Dates*, "by the early Romans not out of respect, but to find out by their breath whether they had been drinking wine, this being criminal for women to do, as it sometimes led to adultery".

Grime and grease pack a punch

Pollution is not all bad — it makes for strong beer and ale. At least that was the belief of the *Brewers' Guide of London* in 1702, when it provided this recipe for making extra potent ale:

"Thames water taken up about Greenwich at Low-water when it is free from all brackishness of the sea *and it has all the Fat and Sullage* of this great city of London, makes very strong drink. It will all itself ferment wonderfully and after its due purgations and three times stinking, it will be so strong that several Sea commanders have told me that it has often fuddled their murriners."

Roman way to lead a damsel astray

Vermouth has not always been only a vital ingredient in cocktails — in Roman times the forerunner of today's vermouth was hailed as a powerful aphrodisiac. One Roman guide for young blades advised: "Take elecampane, the seeds of flowers, vervain and berries of mistletoe. Dry them well in the oven, then beat them into a powder and give it to the party you design upon in a glass of wine and it will work wonderful effect to your advantage."

Answers to Boozer's Quiz

1. Page 40.
2. Page 55.
3. Pages 20,31,33.
4. Page 44.
5. Page 65 (see also Page 56).
6. Page 57.
7. Pages 69, 70.
8. Page 35.
9. Page 52.
10. Page 51.
11. Page 63.
12. Page 59.
13. Pages 15, 21.
14. Page 53.
15. Page 9.
16. Pages 58, 59.
17. Page 45.
18. Page 55.
19. Page 57.
20. Page 10.

TOMBSTONE TRIBUTES

Here John Randal lies
Who counting of his tale
Lived threescore and ten,
Such vertue was in ale.
Ale was his meat,
Ale was his drink,
Ale did his heart revive,
And if he could have drunk his ale
He still had been alive.
He died January 5,
1699.

Ob. 1741
Rebecca Freeland.
She drank good ale, good punch and wine,
And lived to the age of 99.

In vino, veritas

 They say many a true word is spoken in jest – and the same applies to wine. The old Romans knew that only too well, as their famous proverb testifies: *In vino, veritas* (In wine, the truth). In this chapter, some of the greatest wits and wisest men ever to take a drink share the true spirit of the vine with us.

Oh God, that men should put an enemy in their mouths to steal away their brains.

— SHAKESPEARE.

The only way to get rid of temptation is to yield to it.

— OSCAR WILDE.

A woman drove me to drink — and I never even wrote to thank her.

— W.C. FIELDS.

Dean Martin on how to avoid a hangover: "Stay drunk!"

Author Kingsley Amis has this advice on how to cope with hangovers: "Immediately on waking, start telling yourself how lucky you are to be feeling so bloody awful. This, known as George Gale's paradox, recognizes the truth that if you do not feel bloody awful after a hefty night then you are still drunk, and must sober up in a waking state before the hangover dawns!"

"Water, taken in moderation, never hurt anybody," said Mark Twain. But before you decide to drink only water, consider the following facts. To fill a Texas "ten-gallon" hat you need only three-quarters of a gallon of water. A jellyfish is 95.4 percent water, while the water content of an adult human is between 58 and 66 percent of body weight.

> *And Noah he often said to his wife*
> *when he sat down to dine,*
> *'I don't care where the water goes*
> *if it doesn't get into the wine.'*
> — GILBERT KEITH CHESTERTON.

In the order named these are the hardest to control: wine, women and song!
— FRANKLIN P. ADAMS.

> God made the Vine,
> Was it a sin
> That Man made Wine
> To drown trouble in?
> — OLIVER HERFORD

Wine is the drink of the gods, milk the drink of babies, tea the drink of women, and water the drink of beasts.
— JOHN STUART BLACKIE.

EVERYBODY loves
SOMEBODY...

DEAN MARTINI

Dean Martin, a great fan on the odd drop: "I feel sorry for people who don't drink. When they wake up in the morning that's as good as they are going to feel all day long."

A meal without wine is a day without sunshine.

— LOUIS VAUDABLE, owner of Maxim's, Paris.

If with water you fill up your glasses,
You'll never write anything wise;
For wine is the horse of Parnassus,
Which hurries a bard to the skies.

— THOMAS MOORE.

A teetotaller is the very worst sort of drunkard.

— E.F. BENSON.

There was once a man who learnt to mind his own business.
He went to heaven. I hope teetotallers will remember that.

— T.W.H. CROSLAND.

I'm only a beer teetotaller, not a champagne teetotaller.

— GEORGE BERNARD SHAW.

I do not drink more than a sponge.

— French author FRANCOIS RABELAIS.

Author G.E.W. Russell described whiskey as "A torchlight procession marching down your throat".

A good Martini should be strong enough to make your
eyeballs bubble, and so cold your teeth will ache, and you'll
think you're hearing sleigh bells.

— L.G. SHREVE.

*There are two things that will be believed of any man what-
soever, and one of them is that he has taken to drink.*

— BOOTH TARKINGTON.

Scotch whisky to a Scotchman is as innocent as milk is to the
rest of the human race.

— MARK TWAIN.

**While beer brings gladness, don't forget
That water only makes you wet.**

— HARRY LEON WILSON.

Here's to good old Whiskey
So amber and clear.
'Tis not so sweet as woman's lips
But a damned sight more sincere.

— LEWIS C. HENRY.

The rapturous, wide and ineffable pleasure of drinking at someone else's expense.

— HENRY S. LEIGH.

I reminded him of that old saying, "There are more old drunkards than old doctors."

— J.P. MCEVOY.

I drink only to make my friends seem interesting.

— DON MARQUIS.

There is nothing wrong with sobriety in moderation.

— JOHN CIARDI.

'Twas honest old Noah first planted the Vine
And mended his Morals by drinking its wine . . .

— BENJAMIN FRANKLIN.

One drink is just right, two are too many, three are too few.

— SPANISH SAYING.

One swallow does not make a summer but too many swallows make a fall.

— GEORGE PRENTICE.

There are two reasons for drinking: one is when you are thirsty, to cure it; the other, when you are not thirsty, to prevent it.

— THOMAS LOVE PEACOCK.

Men with short necks got no business drinking neat whiskey. It don't have time to cool. It hits their stomachs red hot and burns 'em right out.

— WALLACE MORTON.

Why has the good old custom of coming together to get drunk gone out? Think of the delight of drinking in pleasant company and then lying down to sleep a deep long sleep.

— NATHANIEL HAWTHORNE

———

AS CHURCHILL SAID ...

Field Marshal Bernard Montgomery primly told Sir Winston Churchill: "I do not smoke or drink and I am one hundred percent fit." Churchill, who confessed he survived World War II on "cigars, brandy and crisis", calmly puffed his cigar, sipped his brandy and replied: "I smoke and drink — and I am two hundred percent fit!"

When a fat Labour MP, Bessie Braddock, accused Churchill of being drunk, he retorted: "And you, madam, are ugly, but tomorrow, I shall be sober."

———

A hangover by any other name

Hangovers are a universal phenomenon. Chances are that one fine day you're going to wake up in a strange country with the usual symptoms. To ensure they don't cart you off to the morgue there and then, your first priority will be to explain your condition so you can get help fast. Here's what you say:

Spain: *Resaca* (means "ailment")

Italy: *Malessere dopo una sbornia* ("ailment after booze-up")

Germany: *Katzenjammer* ("wailing of cats")

France: *Gueule de bois* ("wooden throat")

Sweden: *Hont i haret* ("a pain in the roots of the hair")

Denmark: *Tommermaend* ("carpenters")

Norway: *Jeg har tommermen* ("Carpenters in my head")

Netherlands: *Kater* ("cat")

Poland: *Kociokwik* ("wailing of kittens").

Here's to you ... every day

 Drinking toasts started in ancient times as a way to improve the taste of wines. Drinkers each soaked a piece of spiced toast in their cup, then ate it before draining the wine and wishing their fellow drinkers good health (probably because the wine often tasted like poison). Shakespeare refers to this tradition in *The Merry Wives of Windsor*: "Go fetch me a quart of sack (wine), put a toast in't." Here are some toasts from around the world:

England: *Good health!* or *Cheerio!*

Scotland: *Slainthe eh — uit doch slainthe eh laut!* (Hail to you — I leave you with a toast to your good health.) Sometimes abbreviated to *Slainthe!*

Wales: *Iechyd d I chwi*! (Your health in drinking).

Ireland: *Air do shlainte!* (Your good health). Sometimes abbreviated to *shlainte!*

France: *A votre sante!* (To your health). Also *Bon Sante!* (Good health).

Netherlands: *Gezondheid!* (Good health).

Sweden: *Skaal!* (Your health). Also *Din skaal, min skaal, alla vackra flickors skaal!* (Your health, my health, the health of all pretty girls).

Switzerland: *Gsundtheit!* (Good health).

Italy: *Alla salute viva moi!* (Good health — viva ourselves).

United States: *Here's to you!*

Boozer's Calendar

366

Amazing, fun, bizarre, offbeat, odd, unusual, weird, staggering, stupendous, delightful, true and invented reasons to have a drink every day of the year!

JANUARY

1	2	3
New Year's Day.	Famous dwarf General Tom Thumb dies in 1883	Eskimos celebrate Blubber Day.
8	**9**	**10**
Elvis Presley's birthday	Yak Day in Outer Mongolia.	World's first underground railway opened in London (1863
15	**16**	**17**
Sun worshippers holiday among Incas.	World's first full-sized saloon car exhibited (1903).	Benjamin Franklin's birthday
22	**23**	**24**
Asteroid 52 discovered by Laurent (1858)	Humphrey Bogart's birthday.	Winston Churchill die exactly 70 years after hi father (1965)
29	**30**	**31**
Birthday of drinker and hangover specialist W.C. Fields.	Another king loses his head, this time England's Charles I.	End of the firs month of the new drinking year.

4	**5**	**6**	**7**
Siamese twins Masha and Dasha born in Russia (1950).	Edward the Confessor dies (1066).	England's King Richard II born (1367).	Australia's first recorded boxing match, in Sydney over 56 rounds.
11	**12**	**13**	**14**
Alabama secedes from the Union (1861)	Mystery writer Agatha Christie dies	Thomas Crapper's self-raising toilet seat on display.	Queen Victoria uses the telephone for the first time (1878).
18	**19**	**20**	**21**
Movie star Cary Grant's birthday.	World's first women stockbrokers start in New York (1870).	King George V dies saying *Bugger Bognor* (1936).	Guillotine chops off the head of King Louis XVI (1793).
25	**26**	**27**	**28**
American gangster 'Scarface' Al Capone dies (1947).	Australia Day and Paul Newman's birthday.	Wolfgang Amadeus Mozart born.	Much married and lecherous King Henry VIII dies in his bed (1547).

FEBRUARY

1	2	3
William Dean makes Aust.'s first balloon flight (1858).	World's first public flushing loo opened in London (1852).	Tequila Day parts of Mexico.
8	**9**	**10**
Mary Queen of Scots loses her head (1587).	Shoelace invented (1790).	Queen Victoria's wedding anniversary
15	**16**	**17**
Actor John Barrymore's birthday.	Mule Day in the United States.	Apache chief Geronimo dies (1908)
22	**23**	**24**
First color photo taken (1890).	Drinking man and famous diarist Samuel Pepys' birthday.	Nylon toothbrush bristles mad (1938).
29		
Leap year every fourth year.		

74

4	5	6	7
Rock star Alice Cooper's birthday.	Nose improver invented (1893).	Cassanova eats 50 oysters for breakfast as aphrodisiac.	Charles Dickens' birthday.

11	12	13	14
Englishman Geo. Morgan world's first motorbike fatality (1899).	Abraham (Log Cabin) Lincoln's birthday.	Henry VIII's fifth wife loses her head (1542).	♥ Valentine's Day. ♥

18	19	20	21
World's first airmail flight, in India (1911).	Birthday of astronomer Nicolaus Copernicus.	Scotland's King James I dies in the loo (1437).	WW2 RAF air ace Douglas Bader's birthday.

25	26	27	28
Opera singer Enrico Caruso's birthday.	First Aust. made car, a Pioneer, demonstrated (1897).	John Steinbeck's birthday.	Dunlop's first cycle tire fitted (1888).

MARCH

1 David Niven's birthday.	**2** Spaniard finds rubber in South America (1530).	**3** Martyr's Day in Malawi
8 World's first game of snooker played, in India (1875).	**9** Russian space pioneer Yuri Gagarin's birthday.	**10** Australian patents first sheep shearing machine
15 Liz Taylor and Richard Burton's wedding anniversary.	**16** Slapstick king Jerry Lewis' birthday.	**17** St. Patrick's Day.
22 Explorer James Green eaten by cannibals (1766).	**23** Genghis Khan's birthday.	**24** Elvis Presley's first day in the US Army (1958).
29 Coca-Cola invented (1886).	**30** Painter Vincent van Gogh's birthday.	**31** Zip fastener patented (1896).

4	5	6	7
World's first portrait photo studio opened in New York (1840).	Convict launches Aust.'s first newspaper (1803).	Michael-angelo's birthday.	Lassie's birthday.
11	**12**	**13**	**14**
World's first theatrical striptease in Paris (1893).	Irishman fails in bid to kill Prince Alfred in NSW (1867).	World's first reflecting road studs laid (1934).	Albert Einstein's birthday.
18	**19**	**20**	**21**
Houdini makes Australia's first powered flight (1910).	Victoria votes to introduce secret ballot at elections (1856).	Bear tried in Germany for **terrorizing** villages (1499).	Birthday of composer Johann Sebastian Bach.
25	**26**	**27**	**28**
New Year's Day in England until 1751.	First artificial insemination on a dog (1885).	World's first traffic islands installed in Liverpool, UK (1862).	Movie star Dirk Bogarde's birthday.

APRIL

1	2	3
April Fool's Day.	Cassanova's birthday.	Sydney gets Australia's first street lights (1826).
8	**9**	**10**
Abdication of King Zog of Albania (1939)	Roller skates first worn in public (1760).	Safety pin patented (1849).
15	**16**	**17**
Titanic strikes an iceberg and sinks (1912).	Charlie Chaplin's birthday.	Australia's first international exhibition opens in Sydney (1879)
22	**23**	**24**
Lenin's birthday.	Shakespeare's birthday.	Novelist Daniel Defoe dies (1731)
29	**30**	
Jazz master Duke Ellington's birthday.	Hitler kills himself (1945).	

4	5	6	7
Ketch *Spitfire* becomes first Australian warship (1855).	Movie star Bette Davis' birthday.	Word *Telegram* coined (1852).	Matches invented (1688).
11	**12**	**13**	**14**
Convict James Bloodworth makes Australia's first bricks (1788).	First LPs produced (1904).	Gladiators first fight in ancient Rome (264BC).	Abraham Lincoln assassinated (1865).
18	**19**	**20**	**21**
Scientists prove the top speed of a hare is 72 kph (1874).	British PM Benjamin Disraeli died (1881).	Adolf Hitler's birthday.	WW1 air ace the Red Baron shot down and killed (1918).
25	**26**	**27**	**28**
Anzac Day.	Queen's wedding anniversary.	S. American millipede found with 784 legs (1669.)	Mutiny on the *Bounty* (1789).

MAY

1	2	3
Maypole dancing in Merrie Olde England.	Birthday of Russian Empress Catherine the Great.	Speed limit for steam cars set at 2 miles an hour (1864)
8	**9**	**10**
Philosopher Plato dies aged 81 (348BC).	World's first outboard motor produced (1896).	Fred Astaire birthday.
15	**16**	**17**
First official Catholic Mass said in Australia by convict (1803).	Pianist Liberace's birthday.	First poodle parlor opened, in London (189
22	**23**	**24**
Sir Laurence Olivier's birthday.	First steam engine in Australia begins to grind wheat (1815).	Queen Victoria's birthday.
29	**30**	**31**
Bob Hope's birthday.	Australia's first dentist Simon Lear starts to yank out teeth (1818).	Brassiére invented (1914).

4	5	6	7
First motor hearse used, in New York (1900).	Napoleon Bonaparte dies (1851).	Sigmund Freud's and Rudolph Valentino's birthdays.	Gary Cooper's birthday.
11	**12**	**13**	**14**
World's first TV service starts (1928).	Florence Nightingale's birthday.	Birthday of heavyweight boxing champ Joe Louis.	World's first picture postcard engraved (1872).
18	**19**	**20**	**21**
Prima Ballerina Margot Fonteyn's birthday.	Anne Boleyn beheaded (1536)	Income Tax in US declared unconstitutional (1895)	Humphrey Bogart and Lauren Bacall's wedding.
25	**26**	**27**	**28**
Electric bed bug exterminator patented (1898).	Edmund Waller becomes MP aged 16 (1621).	Billiards invented (1591).	James Bond creator Ian Fleming's birthday.

JUNE

1	2	3
Marilyn Monroe's birthday.	Queen Elizabeth's coronation (1953).	Composer George Bize dies (1875).
8	**9**	**10**
France's Louis XIV introduces high-heeled shoes (1668).	Nero commits suicide (AD68).	Ball-point pen patented (1943).
15	**16**	**17**
Benjamin Franklin discovers electricity (1752).	World's first public address system used (1913).	First magazine t publish a photograph (1846).
22	**23**	**24**
Australia's first test tube baby born in Melbourne (1980).	King Edward VIII's birthday.	Grand Prix ace Juan Fangio's birthday.
29	**30**	
Great comet seen in France and England (1861)	Last day of the first half of the year.	

4	5	6	7
French opera star in balloon becomes first woman to fly (1784)	Robert Kennedy gunned down (1968).	Tennis ace Bjorn Bjorg's birthday.	Painter Paul Gaugin's birthday.
11	**12**	**13**	**14**
Grand Prix ace Jackie Stewart's birthday.	US student throws playing card 56.4 metres (1979).	Alexander the Great dies from over eating (323BC).	British horse population reaches 3.5 million (1902).
18	**19**	**20**	**21**
Wellington wins Battle of Waterloo (1815).	Book matches invented in USA (1892).	Tasmanian boozer and movie star Errol Flynn's birthday.	Film actress Jane Russell's birthday.
25	**26**	**27**	**28**
Custer's Last Stand (1876).	Fat, drunk King George IV dies from over-eating (1830).	Philosophical Society of Australasia founded (1821).	Coronation of Queen Victoria (1838).

JULY

1	2	3
Aviatrix Amy Johnson takes off from UK for Australia (1903).	Boozer and author Ernest Hemingway shoots himself (1961).	Cigarette lighter invented (1816).
8	**9**	**10**
World's first supermarket open in USA (1912).	Doughnut patented (1872).	Engagement of Princess Elizabeth to Prince Philip (1947).
15	**16**	**17**
Flush toilet invented (1589).	First airmail from Melbourne to Sydney (1914).	James Cagney's birthday.
22	**23**	**24**
Chi Chi the panda died (1972).	Tulip Day in parts of Holland.	Britain abolishes tax on number of windows (1851)
29	**30**	**31**
Mussolini's birthday.	Henry Ford's birthday.	Cat Day in Spain.

4	5	6	7
Gina Lollobrigida's birthday.	Salvation Army founded (1865)	Russian Tsar Nicholas I's birthday.	Beatle Ringo Starr's birthday.
11	**12**	**13**	**14**
Yul Brynner's birthday.	Julius Caesar's birthday.	Vacuum cleaner invented (1901).	Billy The Kid shot dead (1881).
18	**19**	**20**	**21**
Cricket legend W.G.Grace's birthday.	Count Dracula claims his first victim (1587).	Plastic invented (1866).	Poet Robert Burns' birthday.
25	**26**	**27**	**28**
First flight over the English Channel (1909).	Rock star Mick Jagger's birthday.	Manhattan cocktail invented (1928).	Jackie Kennedy Onassis' birthday.

AUGUST

1	2	3
First pillar boxes for mail (1849).	Donkey Day in Ethiopia.	Pencil eraser invented (1770).
8	**9**	**10**
Great Train Robbery (1963).	Exclamation mark invented (1553).	First dahlia show in Perth (1877).
15	**16**	**17**
Napoleon's birthday.	First department store opens (1848).	Davy Crockett's birthday.
22	**23**	**24**
First movie show in Australia (1896).	Rudolf Valentino died (1926).	First woman jockey, in England (1804).
29	**30**	**31**
Australia wins Ashes first time (1882).	Drinking chocolate invented (1656).	Jack the Ripper strikes (1888).

4	5	6	7
Birthday of poet Percy Bysshe Shelley.	Film actor Robert Taylor's birthday.	Robert Mitchum's birthday.	Mata Hari's birthday.
11	**12**	**13**	**14**
Dish-washing machine invented (1889).	King George IV's birthday.	Alfred Hitchcock's birthday.	Japanese surrender ends WWII
18	**19**	**20**	**21**
Elvis Presley buried (1977).	Aerial pioneer Orville Wright's birthday.	Aztecs celebrate Moon's birthday.	World's first film festival ends (1932).
25	**26**	**27**	**28**
French King Louis IX dies of the plague (1270)	Cleopatra's birthday.	Volcanic island Krakatoa exploded (1883).	Goat's Day in Mali.

SEPTEMBER

1	2	3
First railway carriage with a flush toilet (1859).	Great Fire of London (1666).	Actor Alan Ladd's birthday.
8	**9**	**10**
President Ford pardons Richard Nixon for Watergate (1974)	Fire extinguisher invented (1743).	First circus (1769)
15	**16**	**17**
Agatha Christie's birthday.	Thermometer inventor G.G. Fahrenheit's birthday.	Coin gas meter patented (1887).
22	**23**	**24**
Sierra Leone abolishes slavery (1927)	Mickey Rooney's birthday.	Ice cream first served (1686).
29	**30**	
World's first cops go on the beat in London (1829).	Jack The Ripper strikes twice (1888).	

4	5	6	7
Roll-film camera patented (1888).	First petrol pump delivered (1885).	First cigarettes made commercially (1843).	Birthday of Queen Elizabeth I.
11	**12**	**13**	**14**
World's first TV play (1928).	First steam railway opened in Australia (1854).	Superman's birthday.	Football pools launched in UK (1922).
18	**19**	**20**	**21**
Greta Garbo's birthday.	Carpet sweeper patented (1876).	Sofia Loren's birthday.	First gift coupons introduced, by New York shop (1865).
25	**26**	**27**	**28**
IQ test devised (1905).	Liner *Queen Mary* launched (1934).	Liner *Queen Elizabeth* launched (1938).	Brigitte Bardot's birthday.

OCTOBER

1	2	3
Julie Andrews' birthday.	Indigestion kills Aristotle (322BC)	Jelly babies invented (1870).
8	**9**	**10**
First photocopier marketed (1907).	Beatle John Lennon's birthday.	Potato chips first made (1853).
15	**16**	**17**
First reported horse race meeting in Australia (1810).	Oscar Wilde's birthday.	Stuntman Evel Knievel's birthday.
22	**23**	**24**
Captain Cook meets King of Tonga (1773).	First heart transplant in Australia (1968).	World's first plastic surgery (1814).
29	**30**	**31**
Twins Day in Nigeria.	First daily newspaper comic strip (1904).	Halloween

4	**5**	**6**	**7**
Silent screen star Buster Keaton's birthday.	Picture postcard introduced (1872).	First talkie movie *The Jazz Singer* released (1927).	Motorcycle cops take to the road, in New York (1905).
11	**12**	**13**	**14**
Adding machine patented (1887).	Columbus discovers America (1492).	First paperback book published (1841).	Battle of Hastings (1066).
18	**19**	**20**	**21**
Cocoa first sold (1828).	Poet Adam Lindsay Gordon's birthday.	Jackie Kennedy marries Onassis (1968).	Edison invents light bulb (1879).
25	**26**	**27**	**28**
Al Capone's second day in jail (1931).	Actor Jackie Coogan's birthday.	Boozer and poet Dylan Thomas' birthday.	Captain James Cook's birthday.

NOVEMBER

1	2	3
Michael-angelo finishes Sistine Chapel ceiling	First radio broadcast in USA (1920)	Independence Day in Panama.
8	**9**	**10**
Birthday of Dracula's creator Bram Stoker.	First Jewish knight in England (1837)	Stanley meets Livingstone (1871).
15	**16**	**17**
First rubberized raincoat (1747).	Hottentots celebreate Feast of the Baboon.	Suez Canal opened (1869).
22	**23**	**24**
John F. Kennedy assassinated (1963).	Movie star Boris Karloff's birthday	First jukebox installed (1889)
29	**30**	
26 shopping days until Christmas	Winston Churchill's birthday.	

4 Machine gun patented (1862).	**5** Guy Fawkes' Day.	**6** Motor car bumpers patented (1905).	**7** Marie Curie's birthday.
11 Ned Kelly hanged (1880).	**12** Grace Kelly's birthday.	**13** Bra patented in USA (1914).	**14** Prince Charles' birthday.
18 Scooter invented (1897).	**19** First newspaper color supplement (1893).	**20** Queen Elizabeth's wedding anniversary.	**21** First submarine, built from wood and skins (1624).
25 Premiere of *The Mousetrap* (1952).	**26** First table tennis sets made (1898).	**27** World's first one-way streets, in London (1617).	**28** Beer shandy invented (1847).

DECEMBER

1	2	3
World's first Labour government, in Queensland (1899).	Neon lighting introduced (1910).	First heart transplant (1967).
8	**9**	**10**
Australia's first parachute jump, from a balloon (1888).	Kirk Douglas' birthday.	Nobel Prize established (1896).
15	**16**	**17**
Roman Emperor Nero s birthday.	Boston Tea Party (1773).	Wright brothers fly (1903).
22	**23**	**24**
Angora Goat Day in Namibia.	Swazi Queen Great She Elephant's birthday.	Pre-Christmas drinks.
29	**30**	**31**
First animated cartoon (1906).	Fountain pen invented (1656).	New Year's Eve.

4	**5**	**6**	**7**
Emperor Bokassa crowned (1977).	Prohibition repealed in USA (1933)	Edison invents phonograph (1877).	Encyclopaedia Britannica launched (1768).
11	**12**	**13**	**14**
World's first municipal park (1834).	Shane Gould sets 1500m freestyle record (1971).	World's first motor show (1894).	Queen Victoria's husband died (1861).
18	**19**	**20**	**21**
Mohamed Ali's birthday.	Christmas crackers invented (1861).	Jelly beans first made (1874)	World's first crossword published (1913).
25	**26**	**27**	**28**
Christmas Day.	Boxing Day.	Peter Pan born on stage (1904).	Chewing gum patented (1869).

The Imbiber's Bibles!

The Complete Book of Beer Drinking Games
With 50 of the greatest beer games from around the world—
plus lots of witty essays, cartoons, and trivia—this book is
essential ins every beer drinker's library.
"A classic guide to raucous fun!" Playboy • **$8.95**

Beer Games 2: The Exploitative Sequel
You want more? We've got more! Over 40 new games, more
funny essays and lists, and the wild Beer Catalog, featuring
dozens of hilarious products for gamesters!
"The book we've been waiting for!" Yale Daily News • **$8.95**

To order, send a check or money order to
Mustang Publishing, P.O. Box 3004, Memphis, TN 38173 USA.
Add $3.00 shipping per book. To order by credit card in the
USA and Canada, call toll free: 800-250-8713.

Please allow three weeks for delivery. Books also
available in most bookstores.